All About
DRAWING

Cool Cars, Fast Planes & Military Machines

Illustrated by Tom LaPadula and Jeff Shelly

Table of Contents

Getting Started

When you **look** closely at the **drawings** in this book, you'll notice that they're made up of basic shapes, such as circles, triangles, and rectangles. To draw all your favorite planes, ships, and vehicles, just start with simple shapes as you see here. It's easy and fun!

Rectangles
are used to draw heavy-duty vehicles.

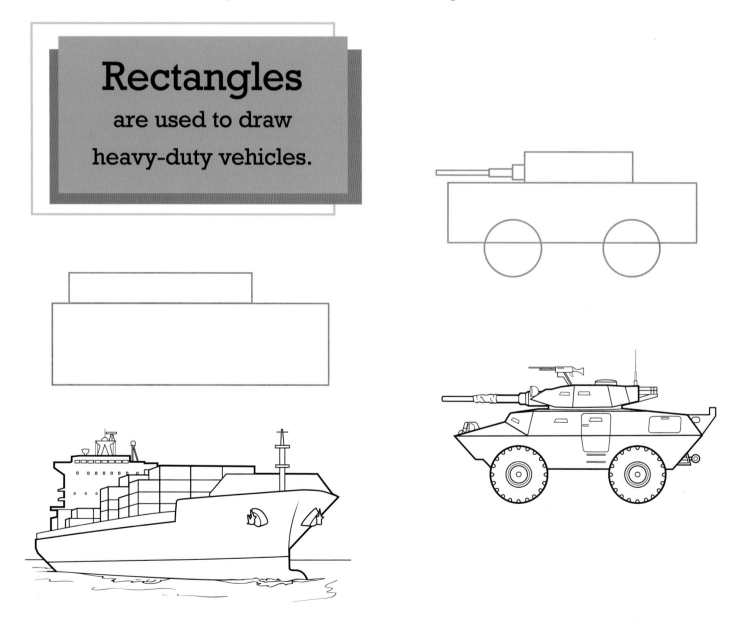

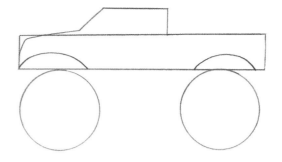

Circles

are used to draw wheels.

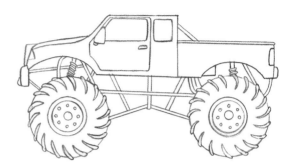

Triangles

are perfect for the wings of jet planes.

FIND THE SHAPE!

Can you find a circle, a rectangle, and a triangle on this vehicle? Look closely. It's easy to see the basic shapes that make up a vehicle once you know what to look for!

Drawing Exercises

Warm up your hand by drawing lots of squiggles and shapes.

Draw a circle

Draw a square

Draw an oval

Draw a rectangle

Draw a triangle

FUN TIP!

There are many different colors you can choose from for your planes, choppers, cars, trucks, and boats! Before you pick colors for your vehicle, think about what the vehicle is used for: Does it need to be camouflaged or should it stand out from its surroundings?

Tools & Materials

Gather some drawing tools, such as paper, a pencil, an eraser, and a pencil sharpener. When you're finished drawing you can add color with crayons, colored pencils, markers, or even paint.

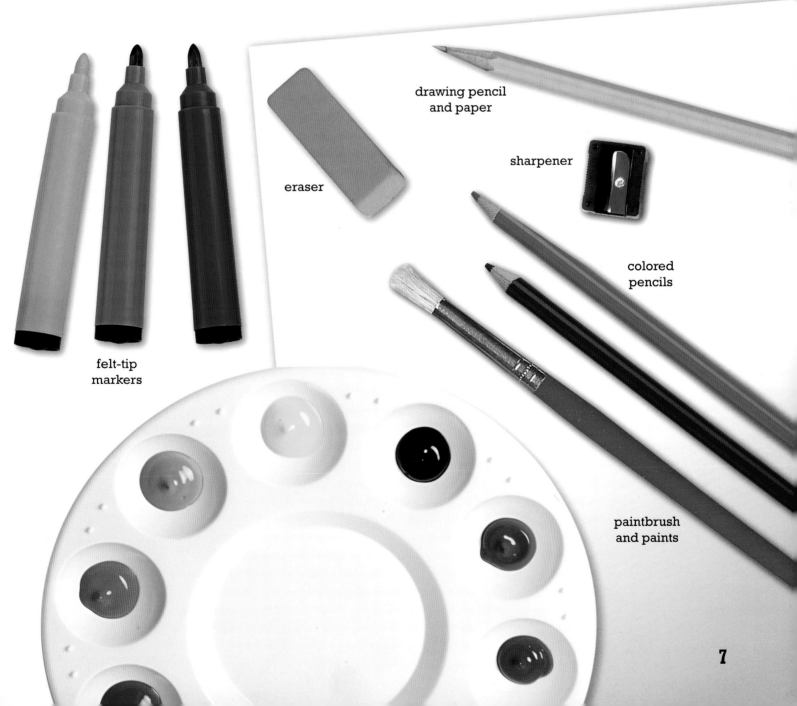

drawing pencil and paper

eraser

sharpener

colored pencils

felt-tip markers

paintbrush and paints

Light Utility Helicopter

This **chopper** is very **quiet** thanks to its covered tail rotor. Giant windows offer passengers a wonderful view.

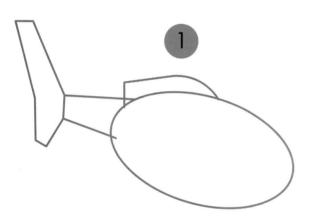

1

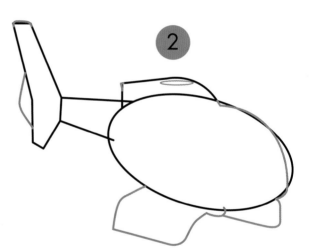

2

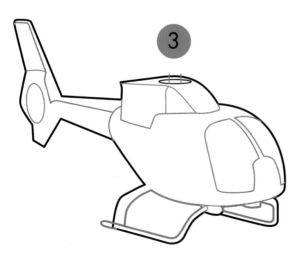

3

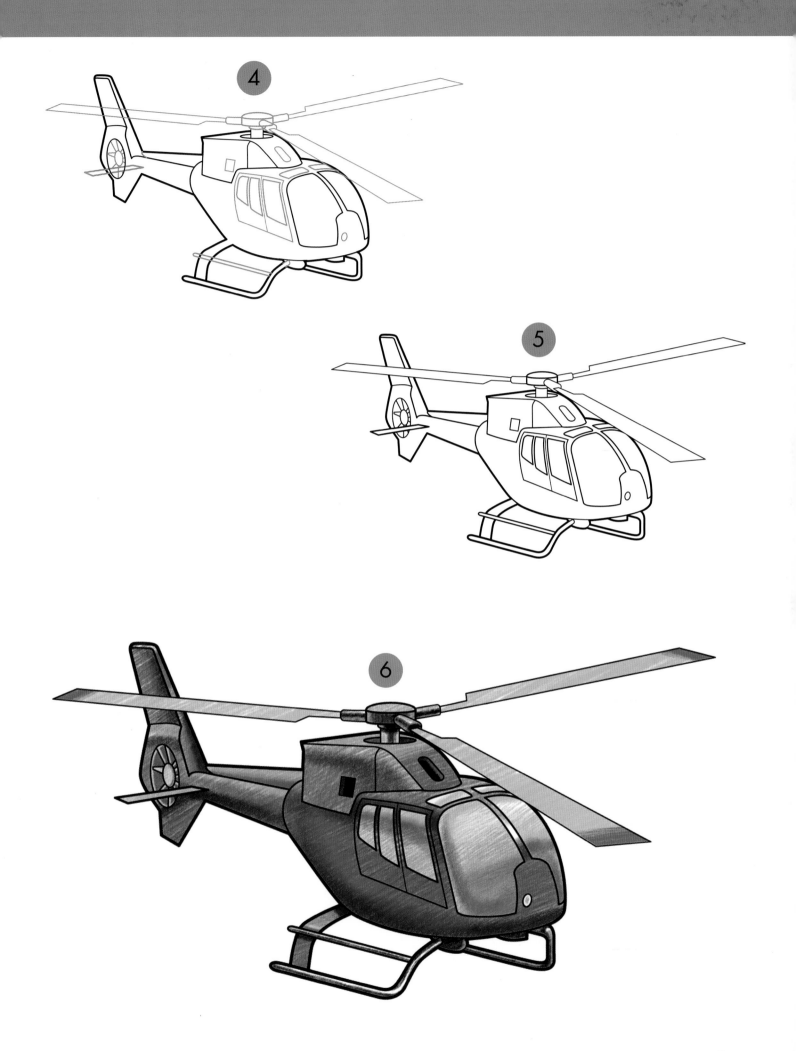

Guided Missile Submarine

This **ferocious** vessel runs on **nuclear** power. It can carry 154 land-attack cruise missiles or 24 nuclear warheads.

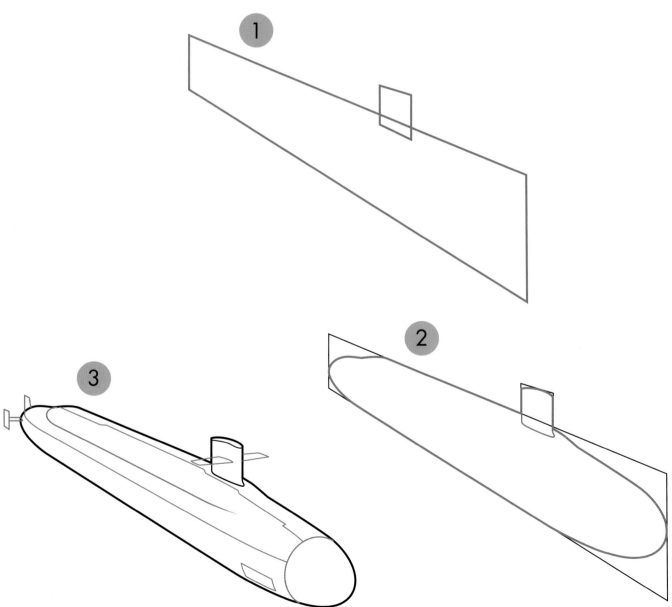

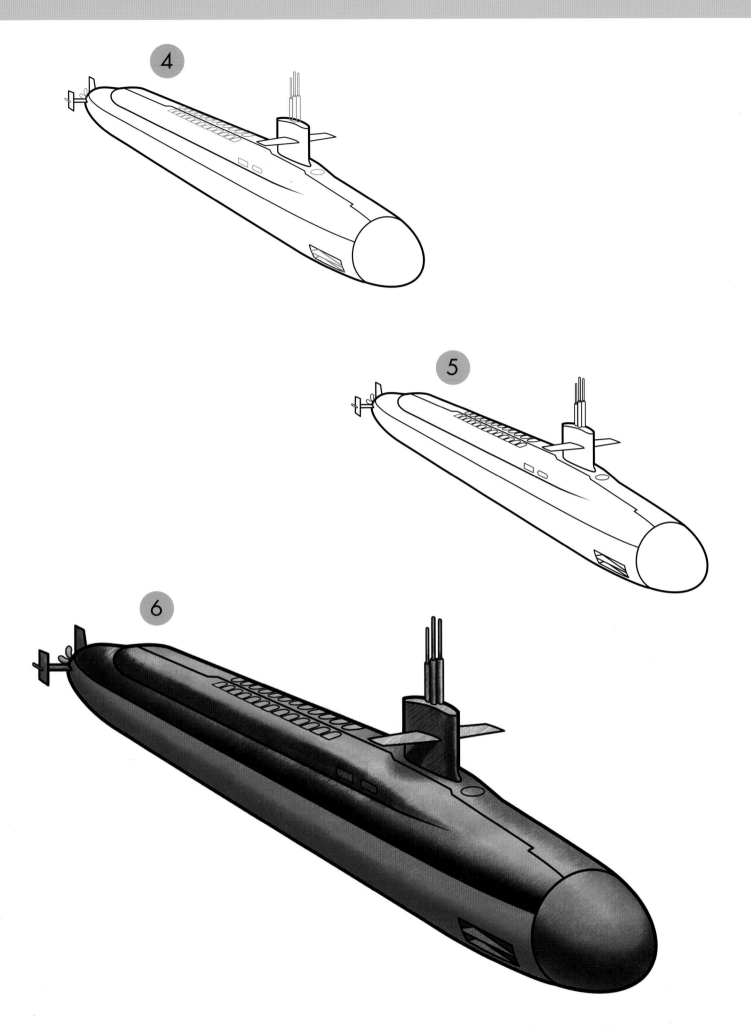

Fire Engine

When the **sirens** are blaring on this bright **red** fire-fighting truck, all other vehicles on the road get out of the way in a hurry!

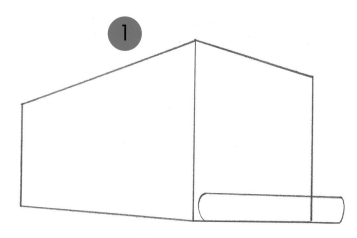

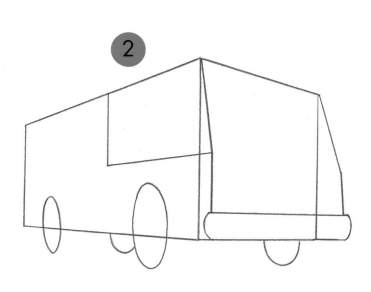

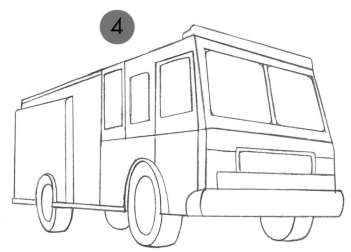

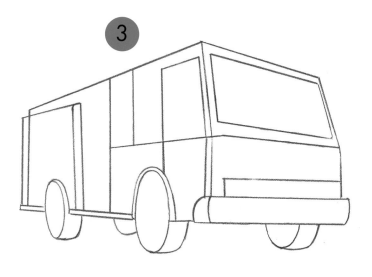

5

6

7

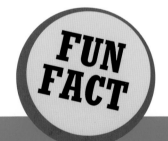

The earliest fire engines were horse-drawn, and dalmatians were used to lead the horses and keep thieves away. Fire trucks today are fueled by gasoline, but dalmatians are still kept by many fire stations.

M36 Tank Destroyer

Used during **WWII**, the M36 featured an **anti-tank** gun that could destroy other tanks up to 10 miles away.

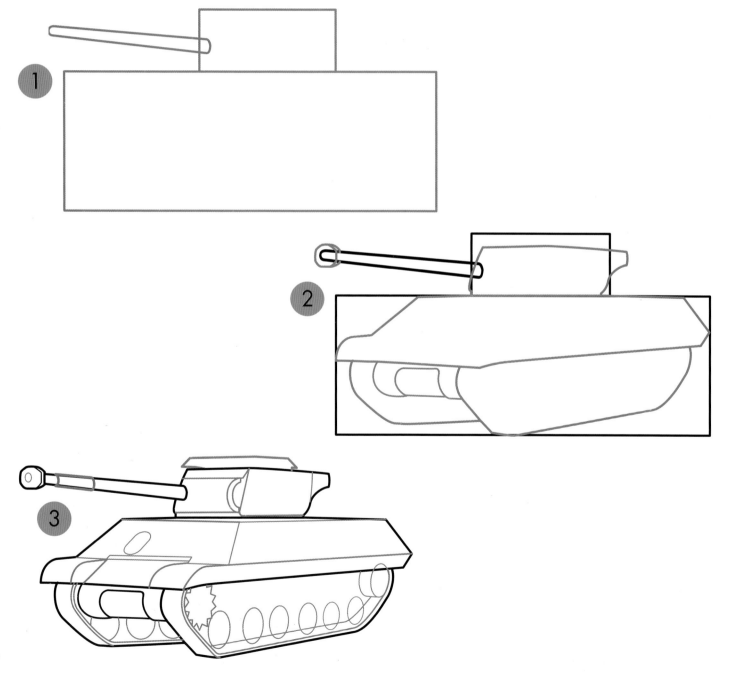

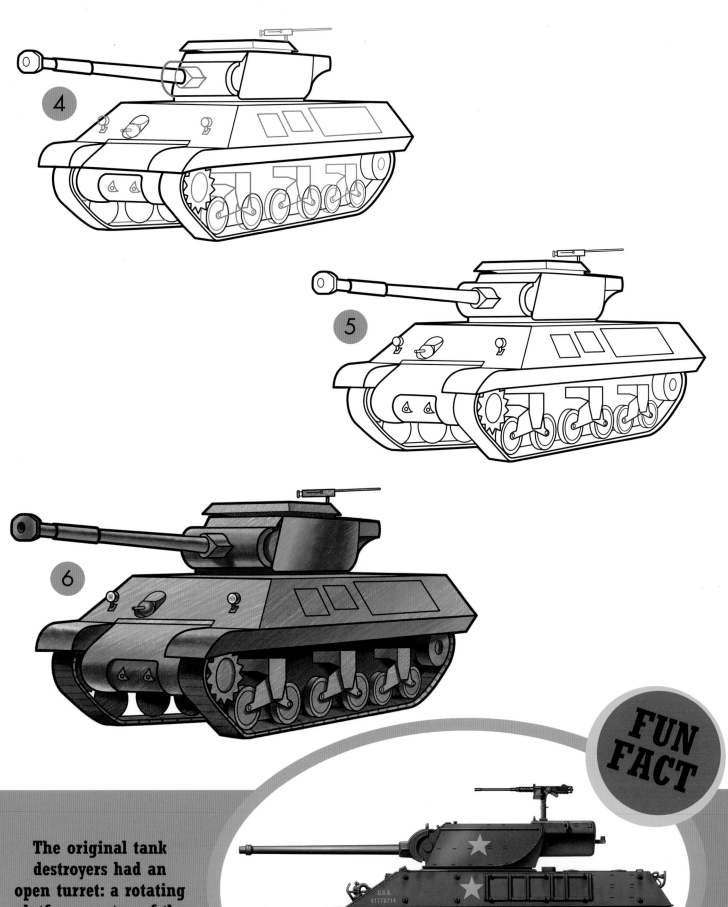

4

5

6

The original tank destroyers had an open turret: a rotating platform on top of the tank that protected the gunner and crew. Modern tanks feature covered turrets.

Twin-Engine Aircraft

This **sleek, angular** aircraft sports six seats and wingtip-mounted fuel tanks.

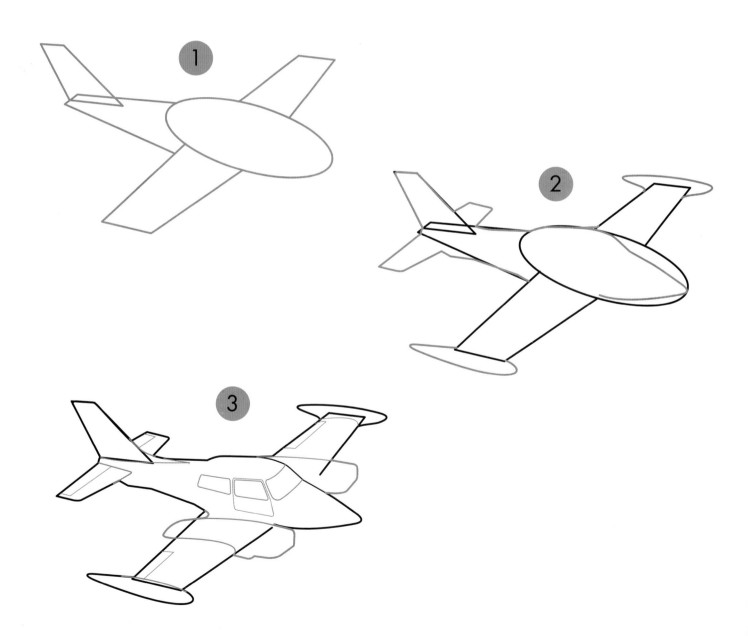

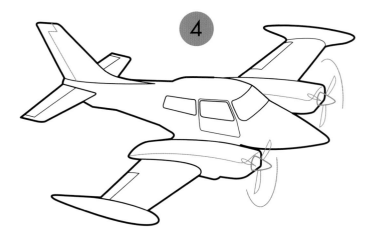

4

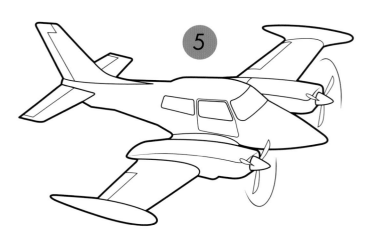

5

6

This airplane can land on Alaskan tundras or in the wild Australian Outback. Special equipment allows the plane to land in remote areas without a normal runway—while carrying up to 2,000 pounds of cargo!

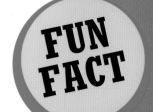

Tugboat

This **tough** little boat packs a lot of **power**.
It can push or pull cargo ships into and out of crowded canals.

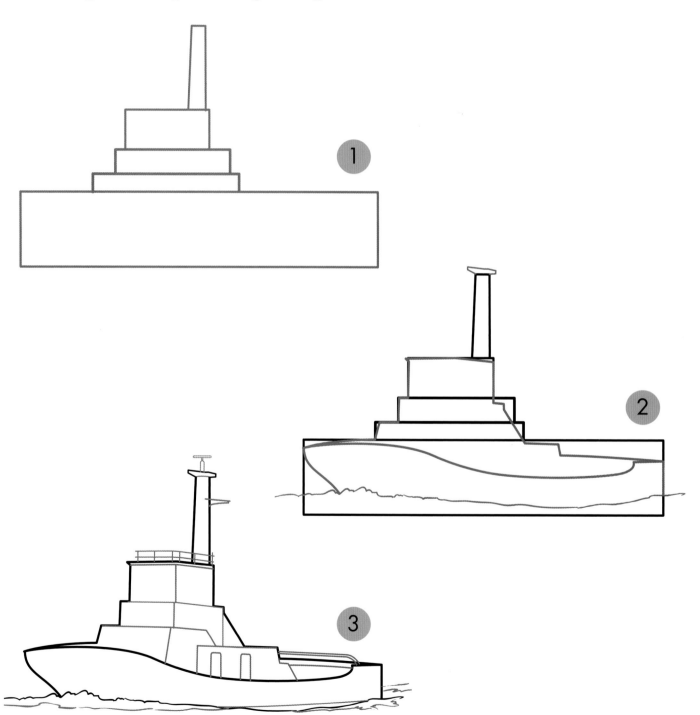

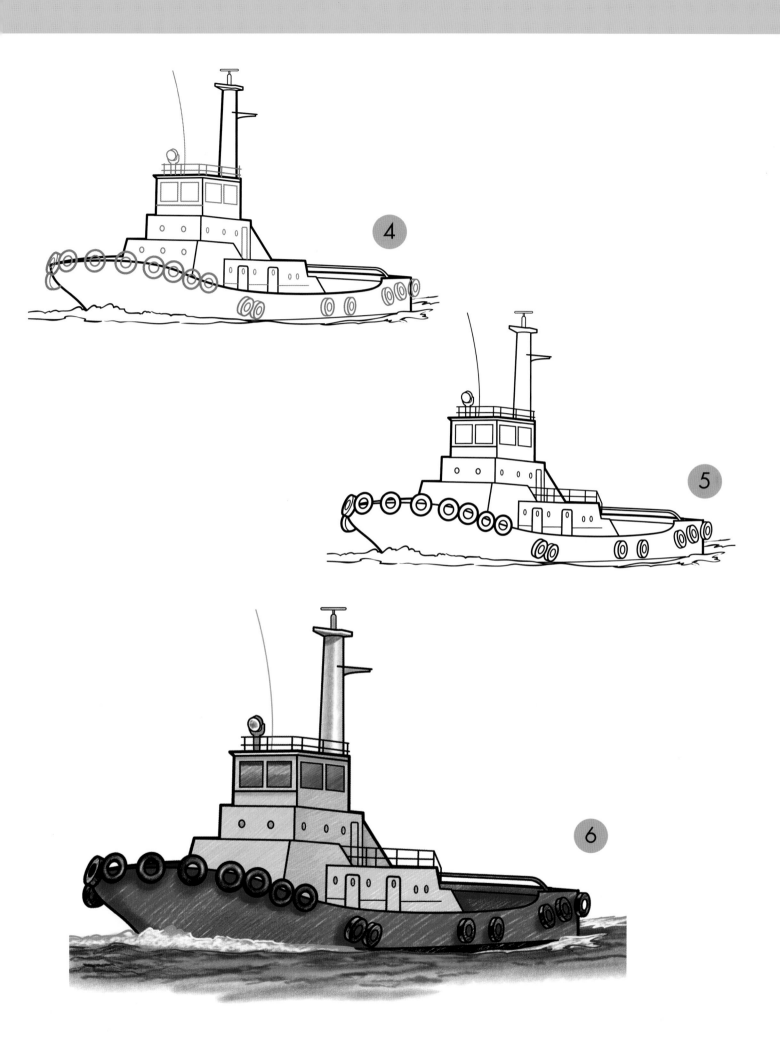

Twin-Engine Attack Helicopter

A **power-packed** chopper with a chain gun
and rockets, this aircraft is designed for close-combat missions.

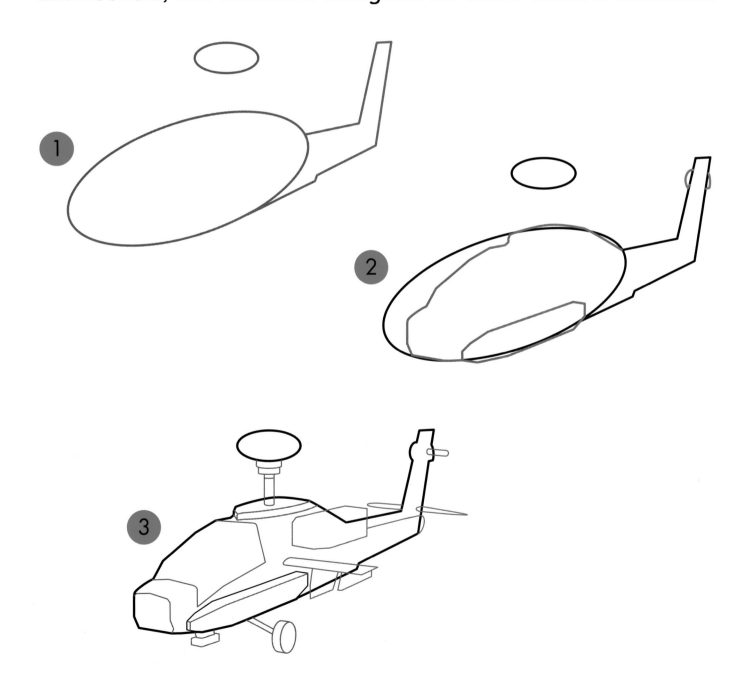

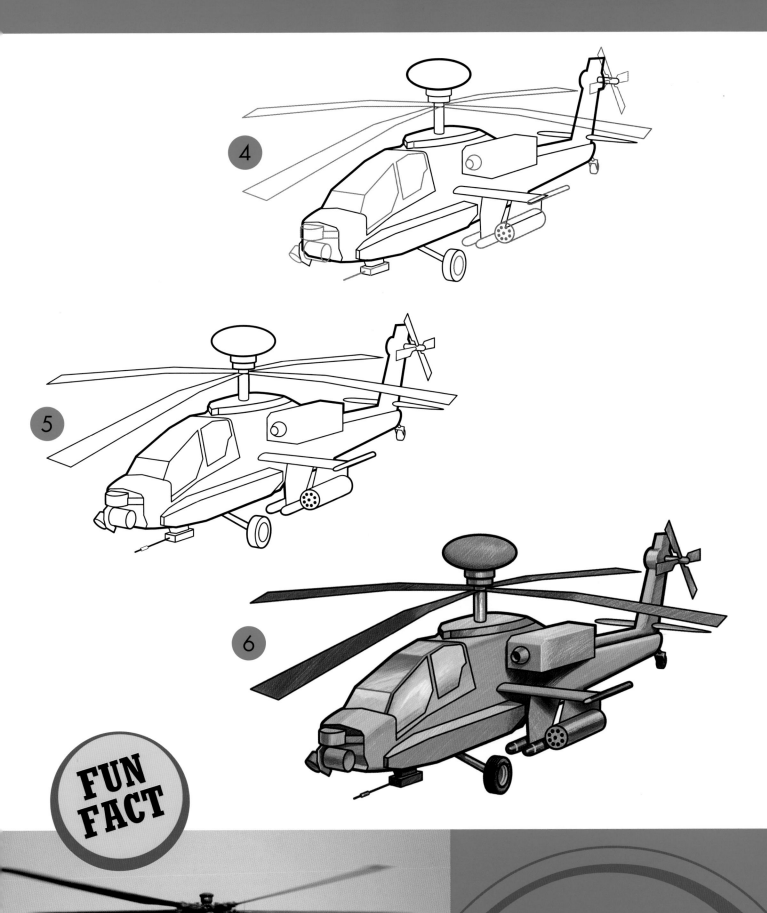

4

5

6

FUN FACT

This chopper's two-person crew can navigate and attack targets using night vision. It can even continue flying after hits from powerful artillery shells.

All-Metal Twin-Engine Aircraft

This **eight-seat**, six-passenger plane was manufactured from 1936 to 1941, but it still flies on occasion today.

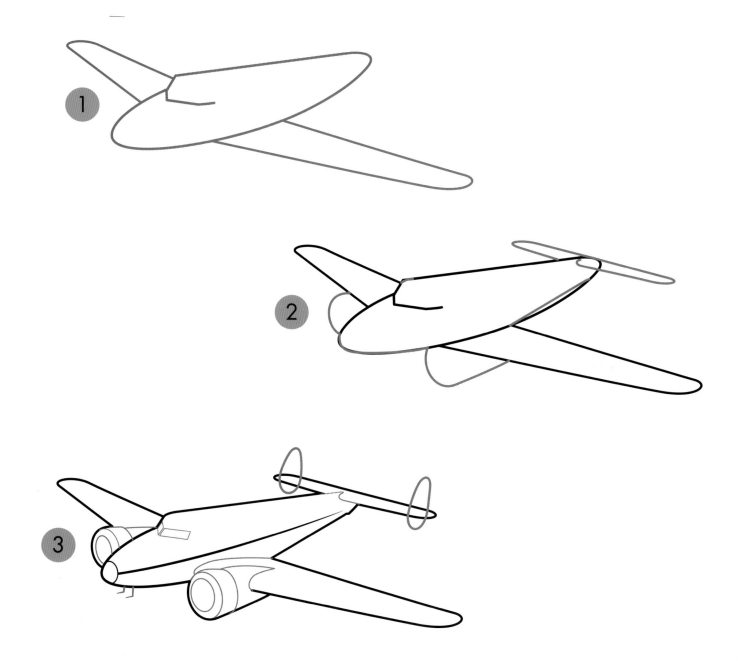

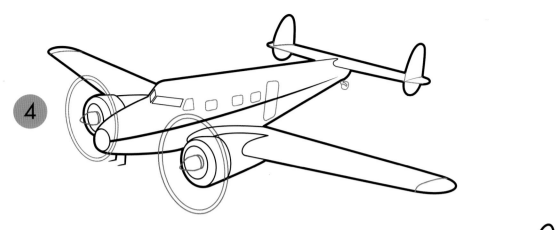

4

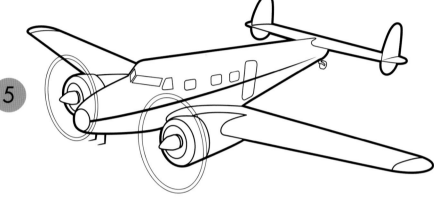

5

6

Monster Truck

This tall truck has **giant wheels** that allow it to crawl over humongous obstacles—including piles of other cars!

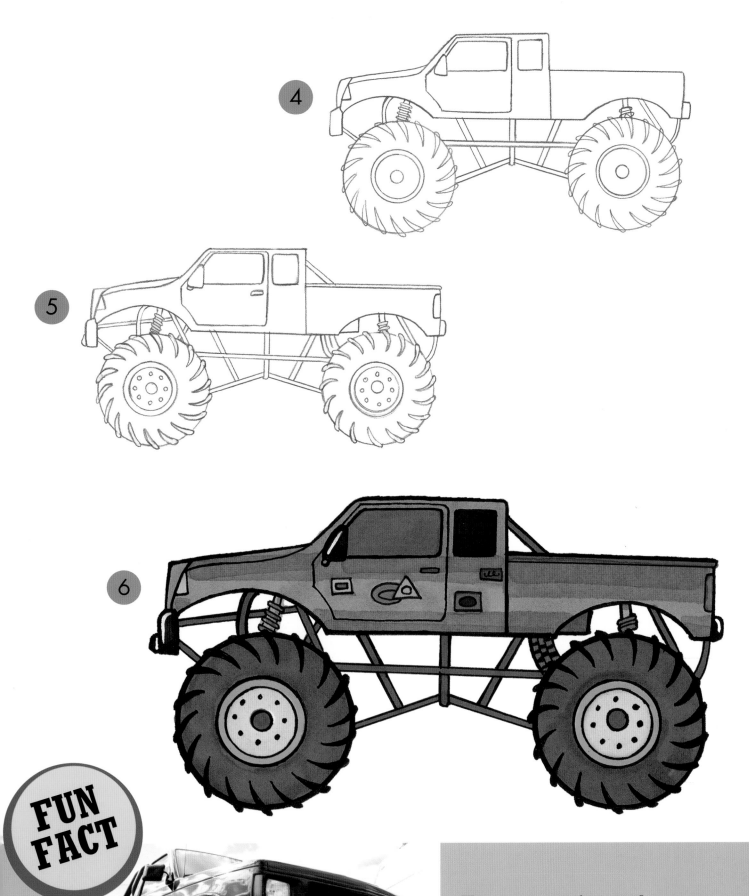

FUN FACT

The enormous tires used to create monster trucks are even bigger than you might imagine—each tire is usually more than 60 inches tall and 40 inches wide.

Medium-Lift Transport Helicopter

This **twin-engine** chopper can be modified to perform many different tasks, including helping to fight fires!

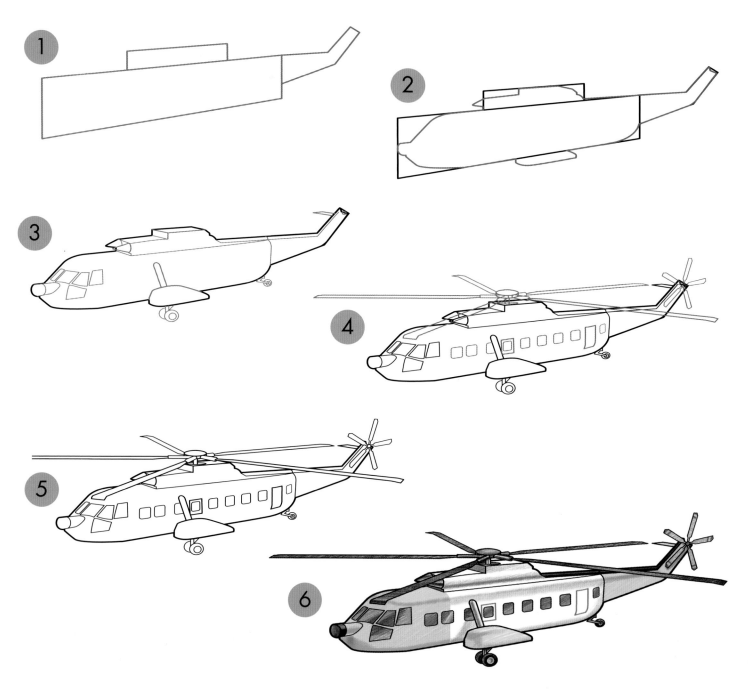

Hovercraft

This rectangular craft can **jet** across **ice**, **snow**, and water. It uses high-speed fans to create an air cushion underneath its rubber sides—it literally floats on air!

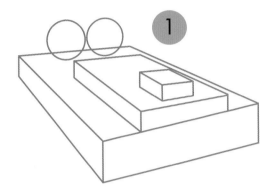

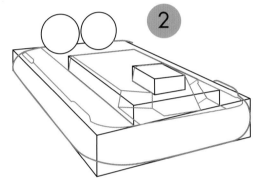

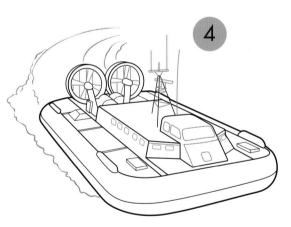

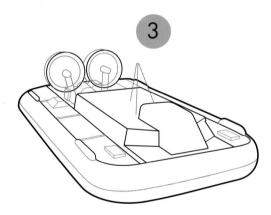

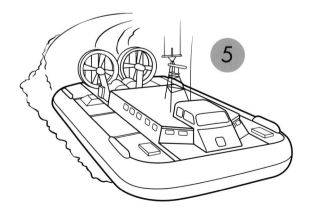

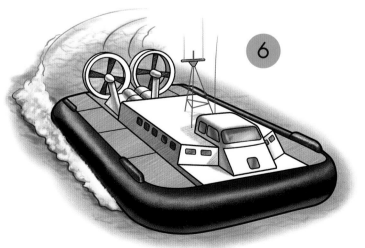

Jumbo Jet

This **double-decker** aircraft has four engines.
It can carry 500 people and travel 8,000 miles in one trip.

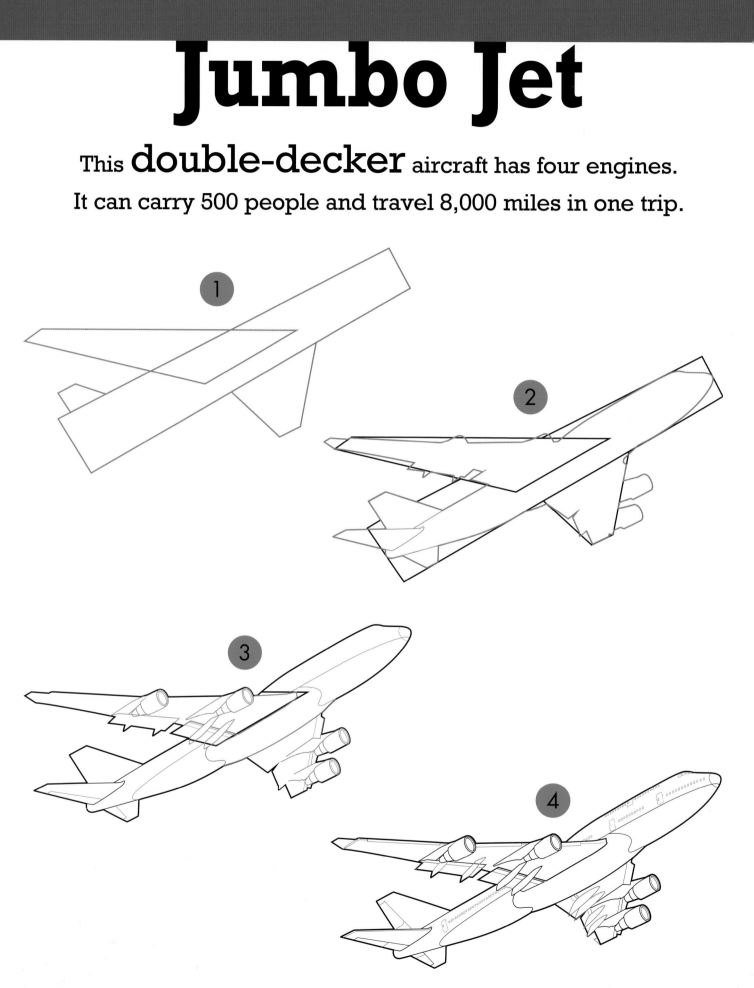

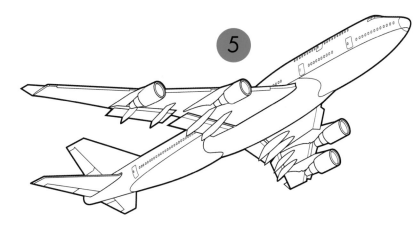

5

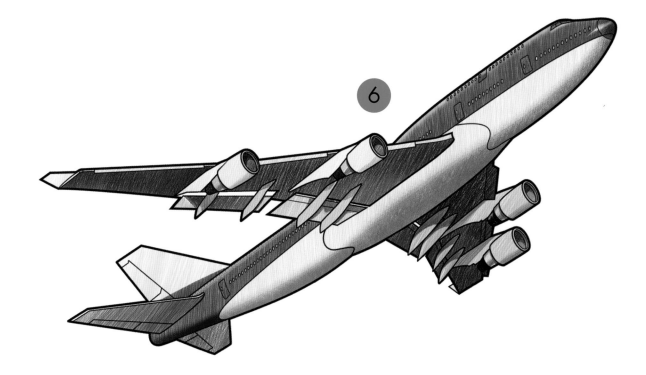

6

This jumbo jet is so gigantic that its manufacturer had to build a special factory for it. It has its own special airplane that flies big pieces of the jet to the production plant.

Four-Wheel-Drive Utility Vehicle

This **open-air** vehicle was the U.S. Military's go-to truck for decades. It was retired from duty in the mid-1980s.

Twin-Propeller Airliner

Manufactured from 1934 to 1937, this **aluminum** plane could seat 14 people and travel 1,000 miles in one trip.

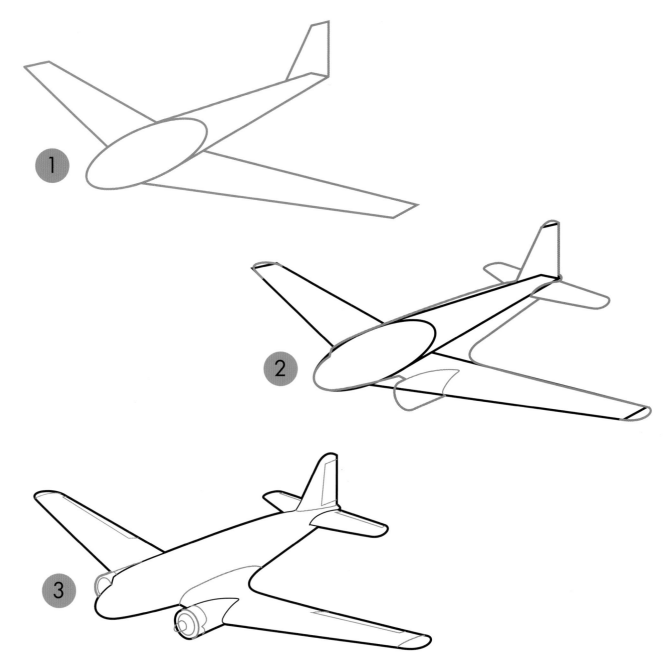

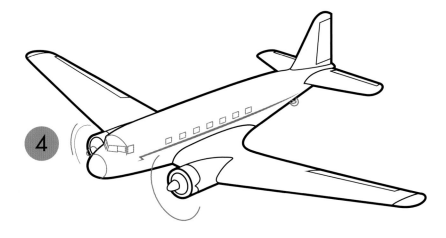

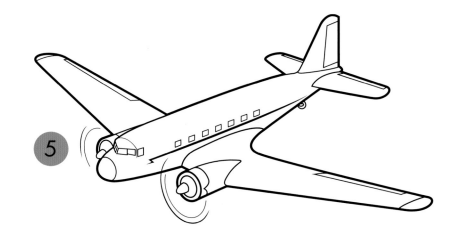

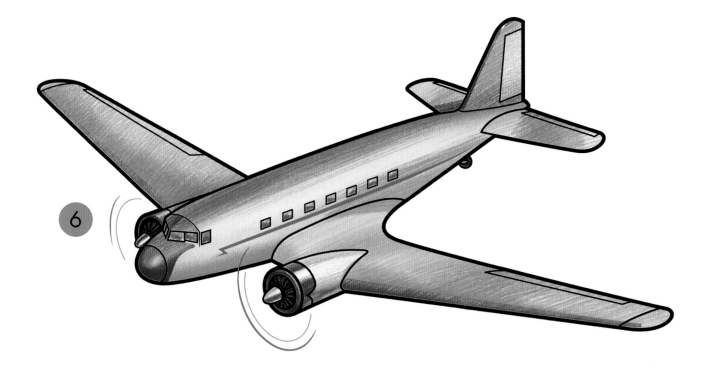

Polar Research Vessel

This powerful ship **rams** through **ice** up to 6 feet thick! Its steel hull acts like a sledgehammer, floating up onto ice and crushing it with a 13,000-ton weight.

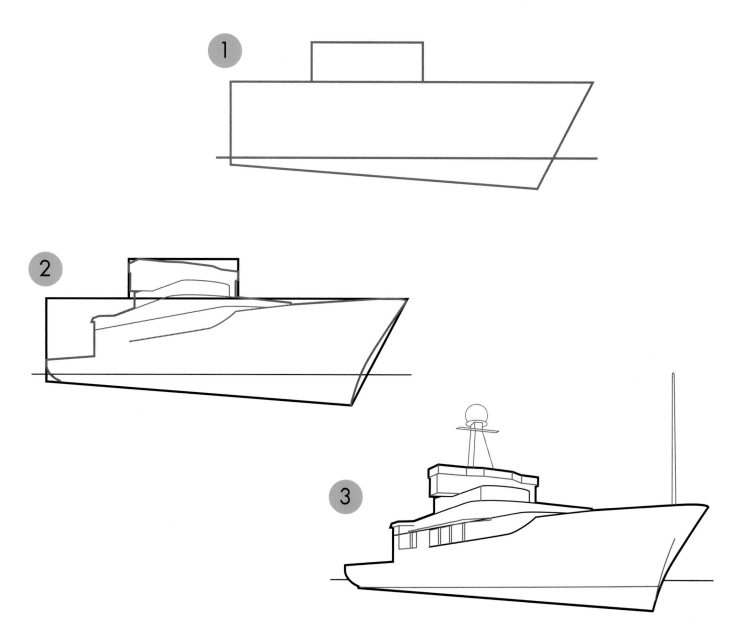

FUN FACT

Early polar research vessels were built of wood with bands of iron wrapped around their hulls to break ice. Later, steam-powered versions used paddles to crush the frozen waters. Modern versions run on multiple gas and diesel-electric engines, and some even use nuclear reactors!

Dually Truck

This tough vehicle has **four rear wheels**, giving it extra weight-bearing power for carrying heavy loads in its bed.

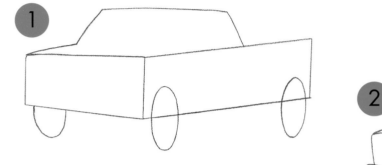

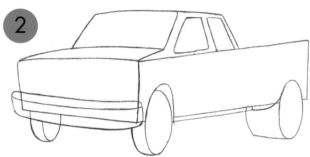

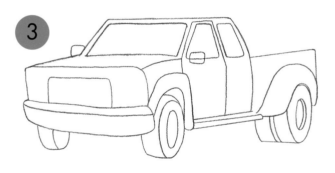

Extreme ATV

This **rugged** and **angular** truck goes all-terrain. It can trek over any type of land— sand, swamp, or stone!

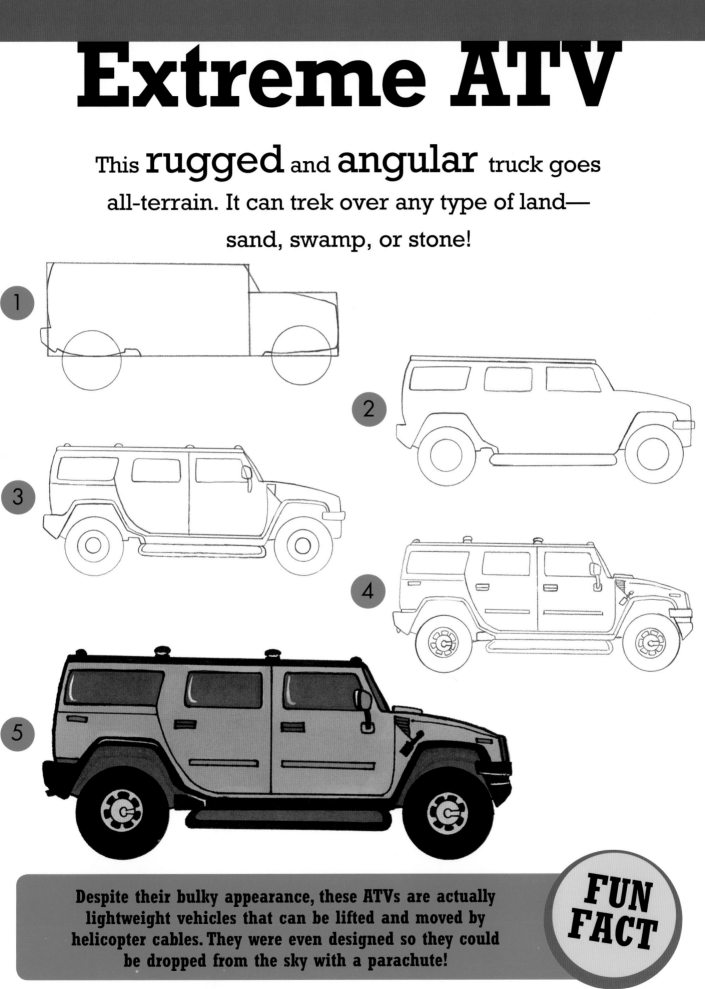

Despite their bulky appearance, these ATVs are actually lightweight vehicles that can be lifted and moved by helicopter cables. They were even designed so they could be dropped from the sky with a parachute!

FUN FACT

Military Transport Aircraft

This plane carries **troops** and **equipment** thousands of miles across the ocean. It can haul up to 500,000 pounds!

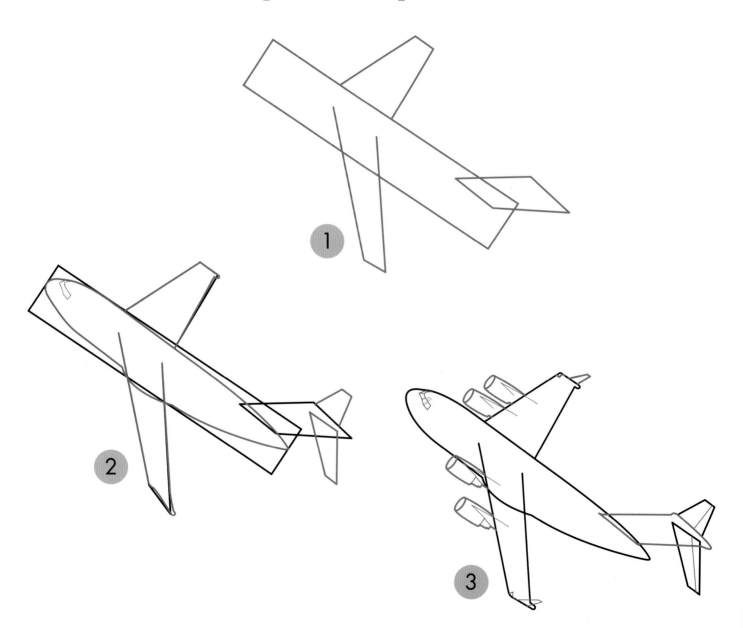

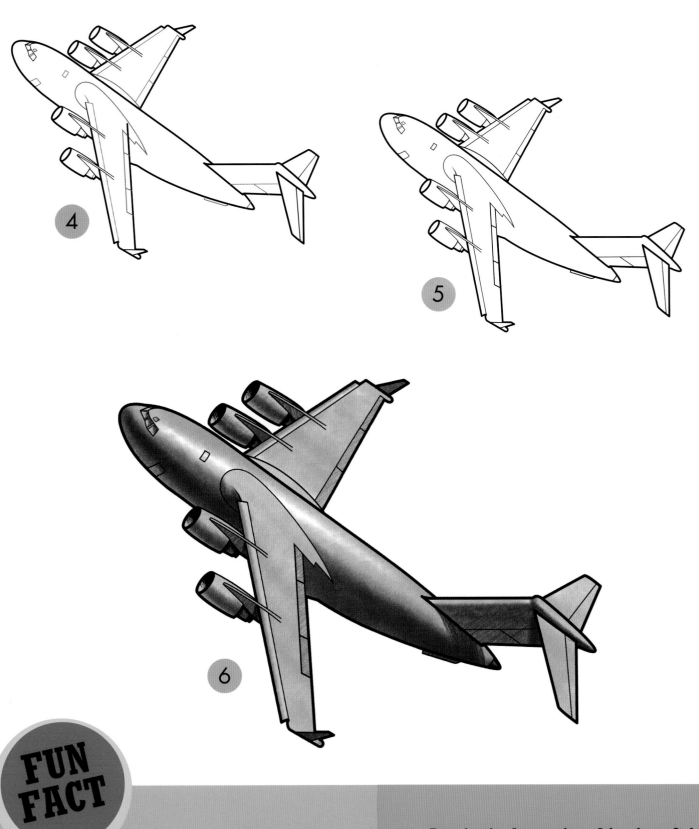

4

5

6

Despite its large size, this aircraft is designed to land on short runways quickly and efficiently. A three-person crew helps load cargo and troops through a rear ramp. Tanks and trucks simply drive right into it!

Nuclear-Powered Supercarrier

This **enormous** ship is used as a **portable** flight deck for up to 85 airplanes. Its flat deck is also a giant runway.

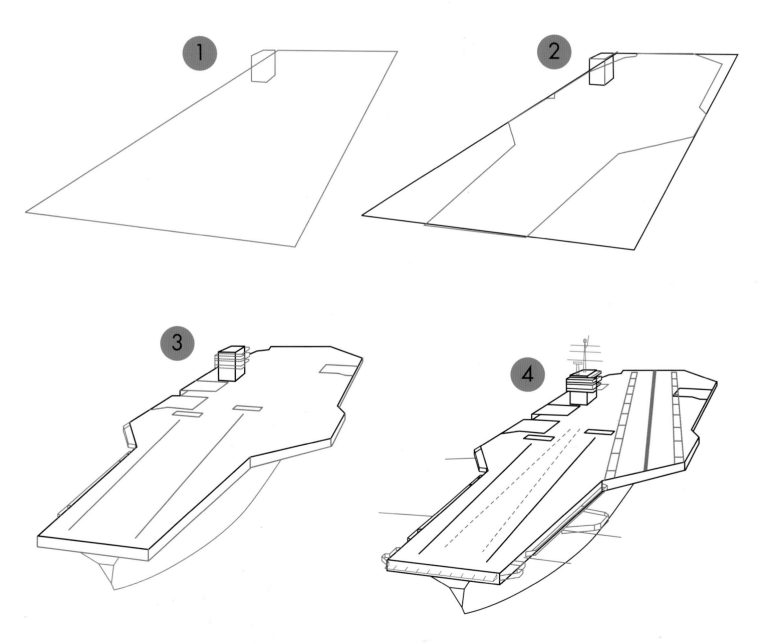

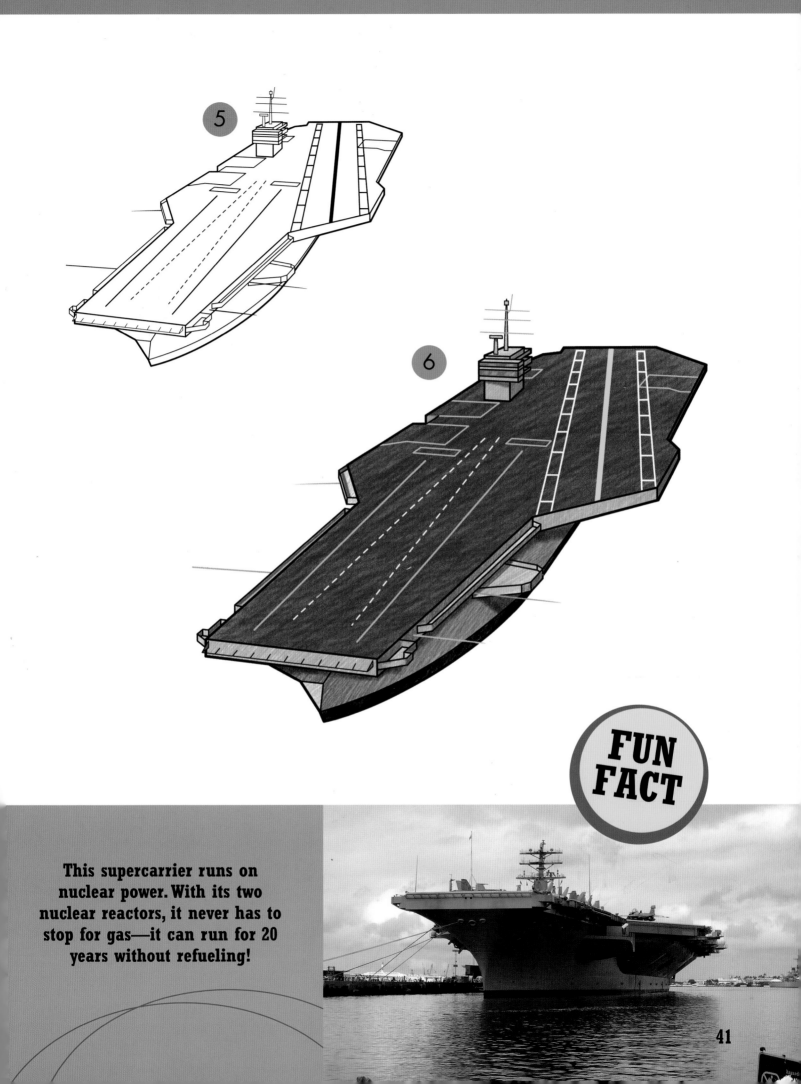

5

6

FUN FACT

This supercarrier runs on nuclear power. With its two nuclear reactors, it never has to stop for gas—it can run for 20 years without refueling!

Light Aerobatic Biplane

This plane can perform **tricks**, including **spinning** in a roll, looping in a figure 8, and flying upside down!

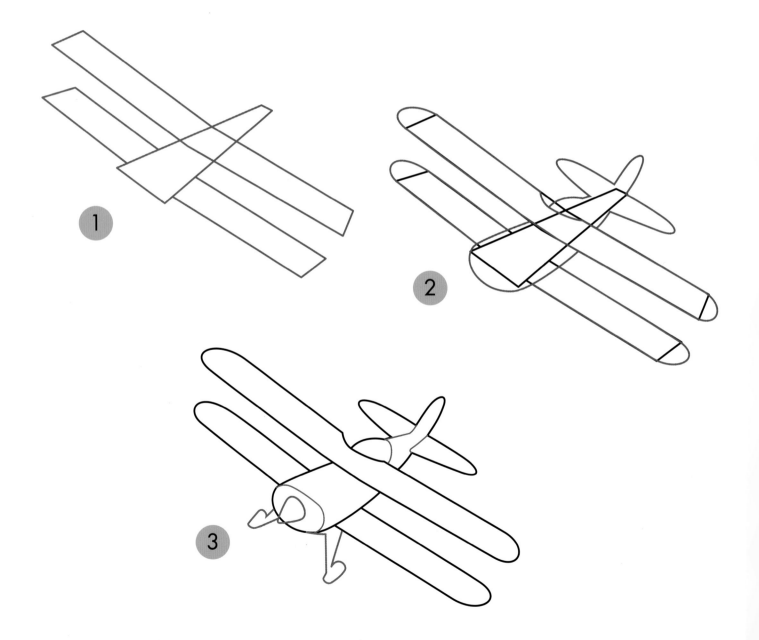

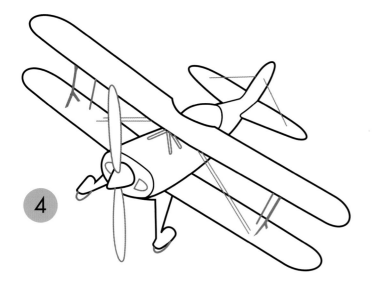

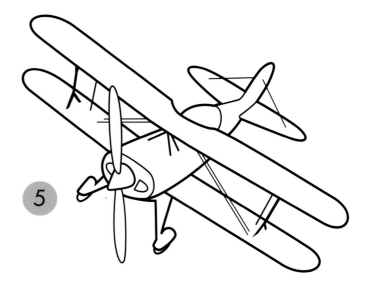

4

5

6

FUN FACT

Since 1944, this double-winged plane
has won hundreds of aerobatic
competitions around the world.
Adventurous pilots are so proud of their
speedy machines that they decorate
them in fancy designs and colors.

Convertible

This **sleek** and **sporty** car has a top that folds flat, so you can use a simple rectangle for a speedy start!

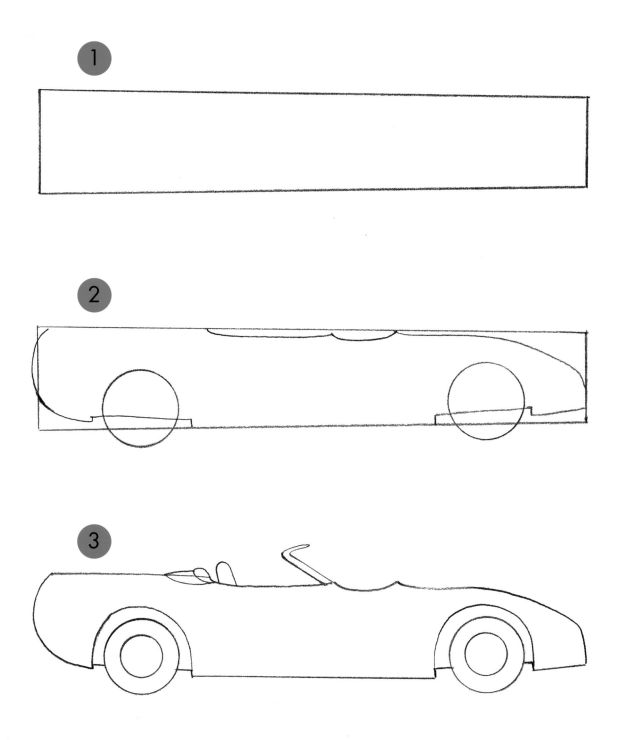

4

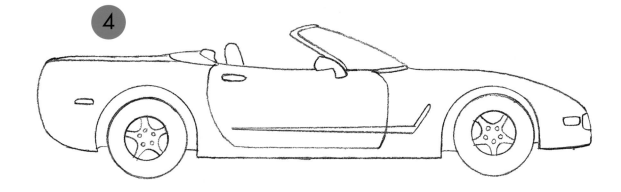

5

FUN
FACT

The first "power top" convertible was
introduced in 1939, starting an open-
air craze that lasted 30 years. But
automakers retired these cars in the
'70s because of new regulations and
safety concerns. The cars returned
with improvements in 1982.

Stealth Fighter Jet

This **sneak-attack** jet may look bizarre, but its triangular shape helps it escape radar detection.

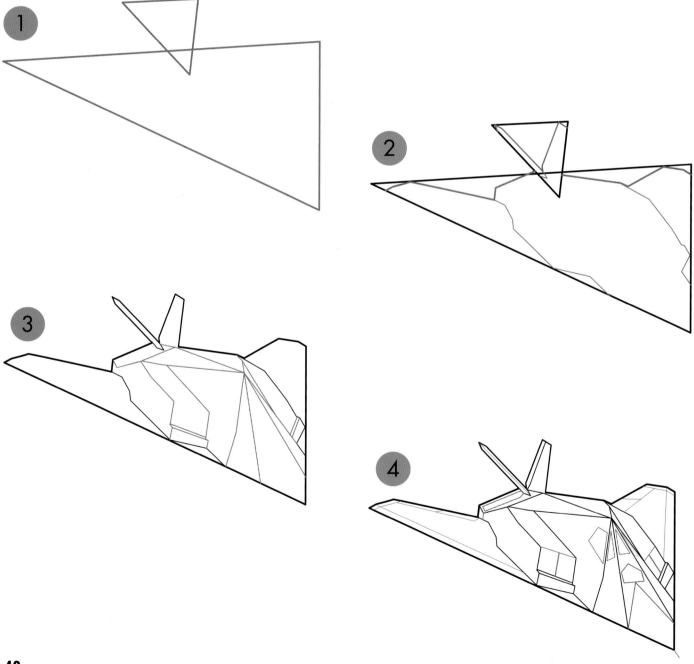

5

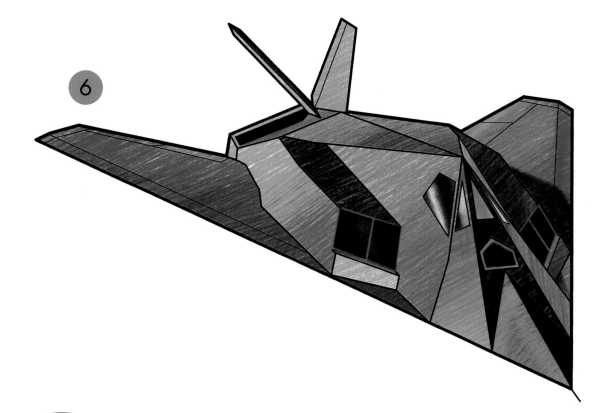

6

This fighter is sometimes called the "Frisbee" or the "Wobblin' Goblin." Despite its ability to fly "under the radar," the aircraft was retired in 2008.

Stock Racecar

The back of this car sports a **spoiler**—an upward swoop at the tip—to keep the rear end from lifting at high speeds!

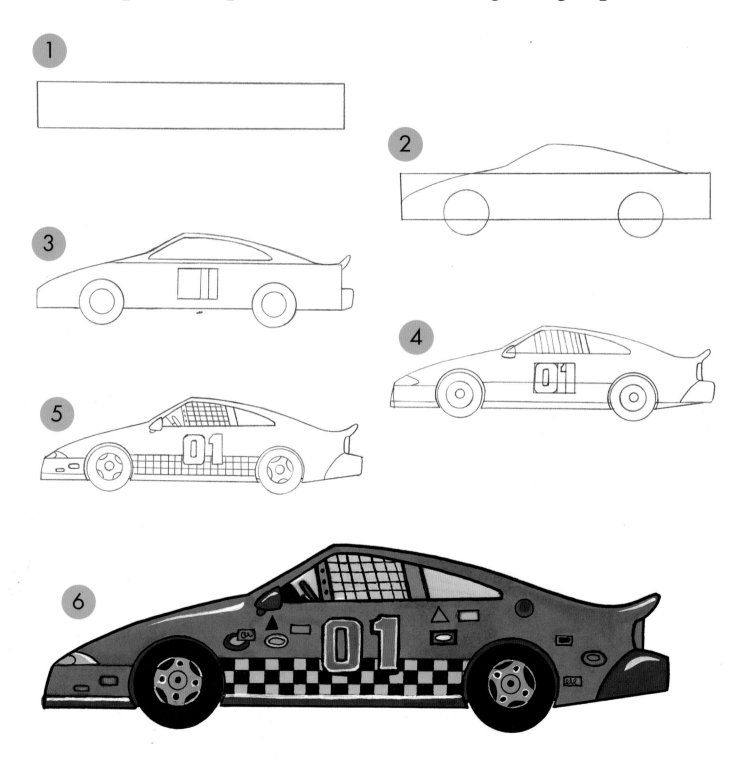

Drag Racecar

This hot rod is shaped like a thin **arrowhead**, so it can cut through the air and accelerate with amazing speed!

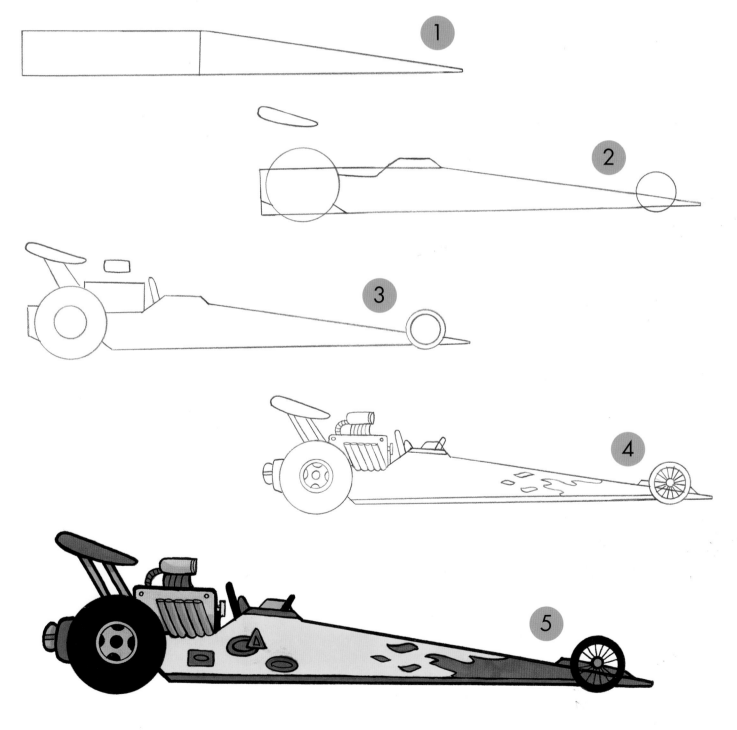

Tilt-Rotor Vertical/ Short Takeoff & Landing Aircraft

The bulky gray aircraft is a real-life transformer:
It can turn itself into an airplane AND a helicopter.

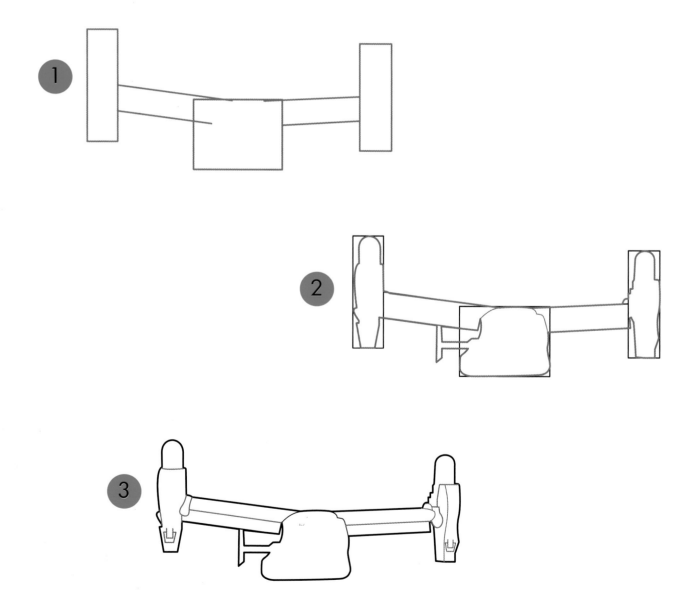

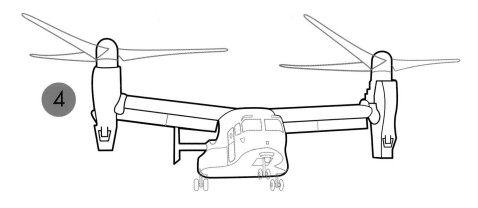

4

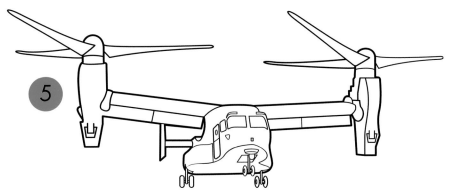

5

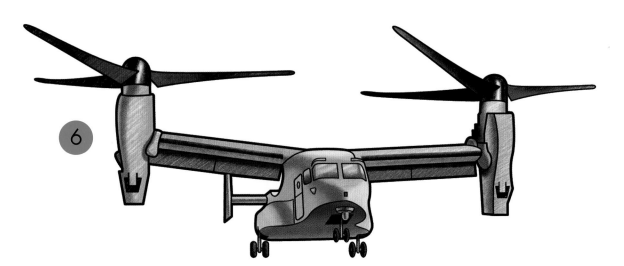

6

This helicopter can do things planes only dream about. Like a helicopter, it can carry up to 15,000 pounds of cargo on two external hooks, and it can take off and land without a runway. Like a plane, it's able to cruise 30,000 feet above sea level for more than 2,000 miles—without refueling!

Short Takeoff & Landing Aircraft

First manufactured in 1951, this plane is capable
of landing on both snow and water.

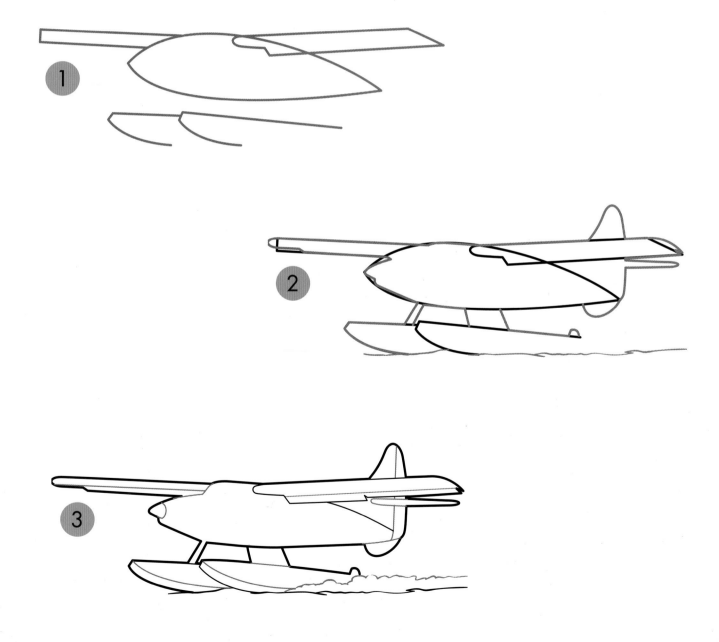

4

5

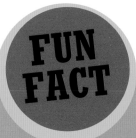

6

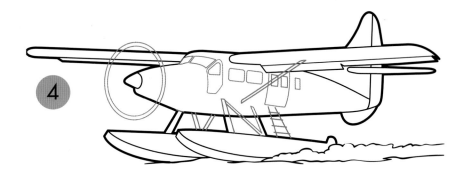

F-14

This **fighter jet** can carry up to 13,000 pounds of missiles. At the touch of a button, the pilot can change the angle of its wings to make it fly faster or slower.

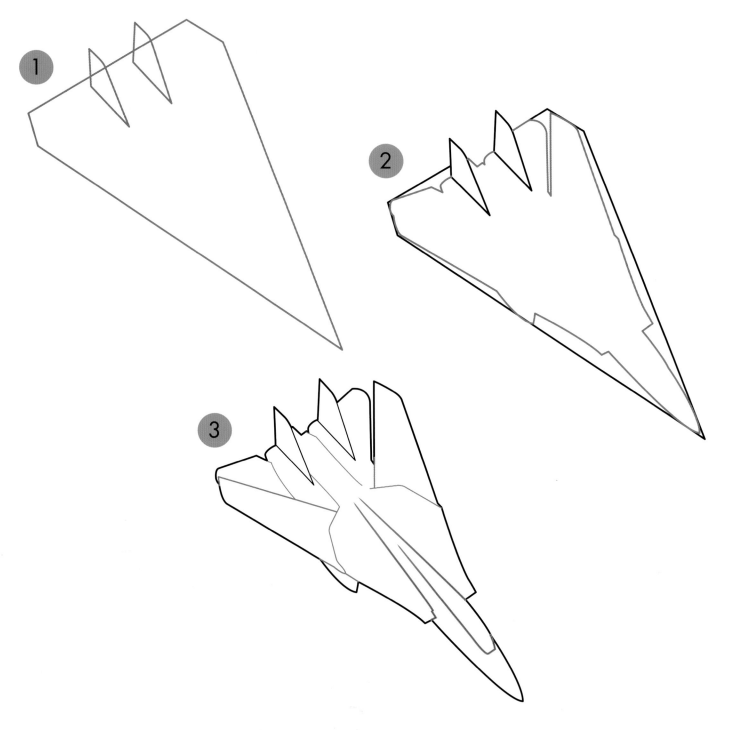

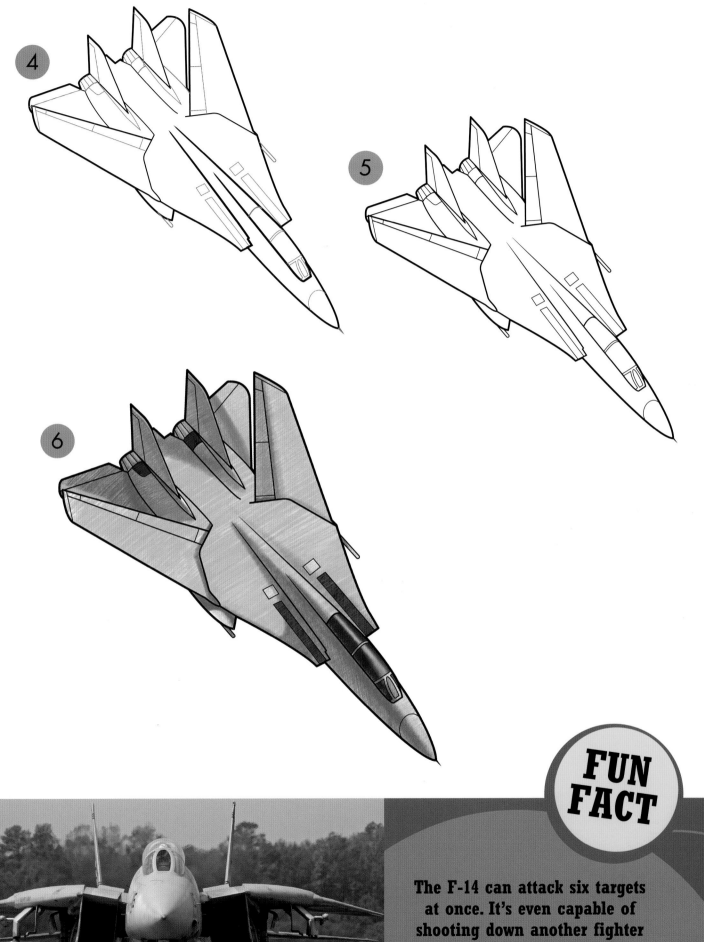

The F-14 can attack six targets
at once. It's even capable of
shooting down another fighter
plane or a cruise missile.

Police Car

Patrol cars are easy to identify. This one's white and dark markings follow a distinct, law-abiding pattern.

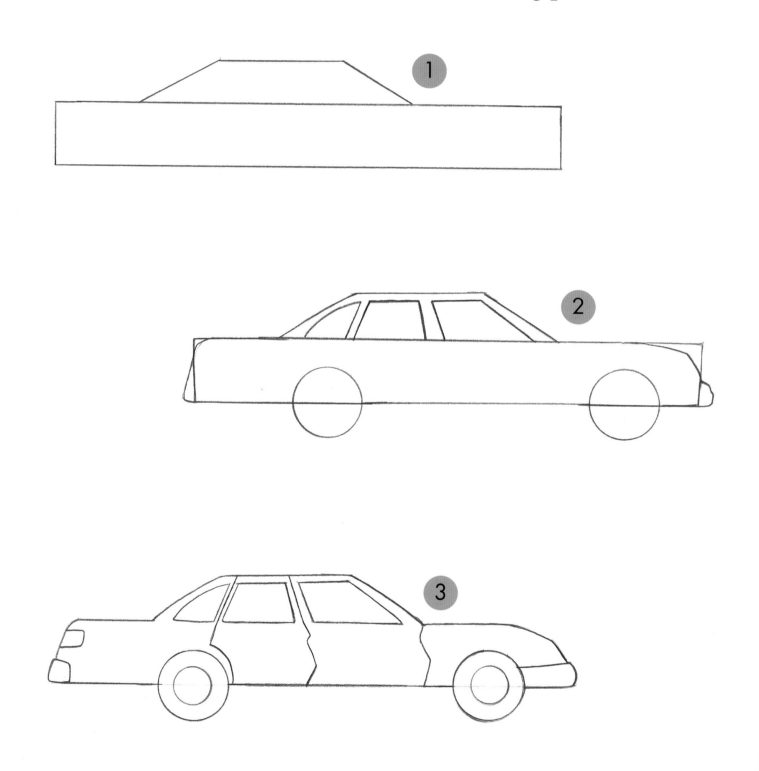

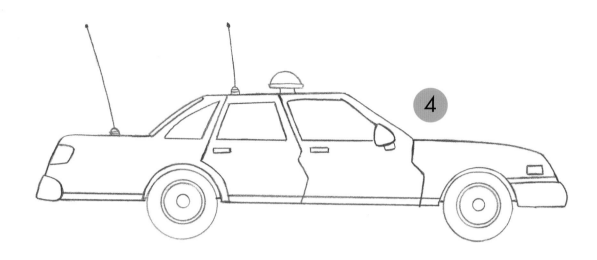

4

5

Black Hawk Twin-Engine Helicopter

With its **three-person** crew, the Black Hawk can transport a fully equipped 11-man infantry squad.

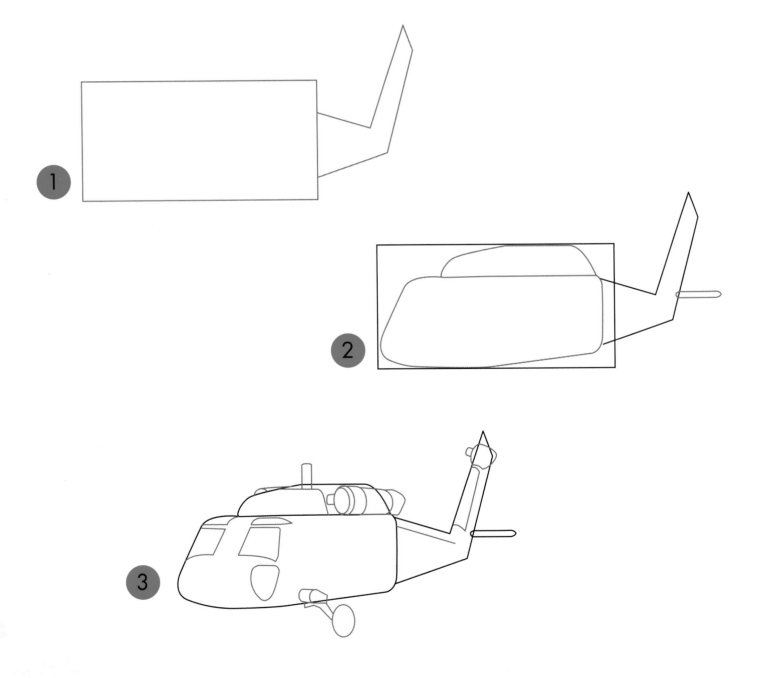

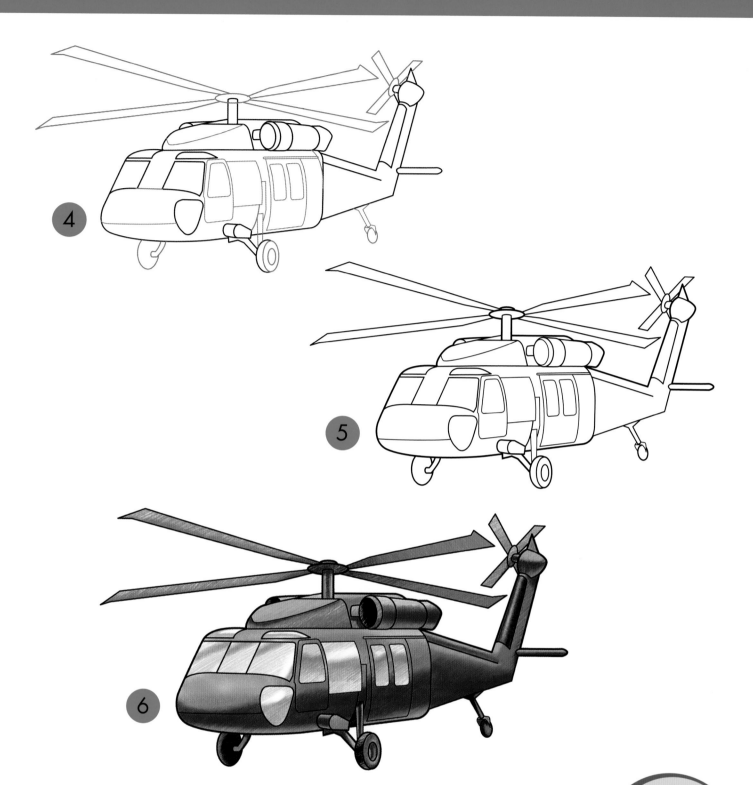

4

5

6

A multifaceted war machine, Black Hawks have two machine guns fitted to their doors and can withstand hits from heavy artillery.

Stretch Limousine

The **long, roomy** limousine allows people to ride in luxury. With TVs, chauffeurs, and more, these cars make you feel like a star!

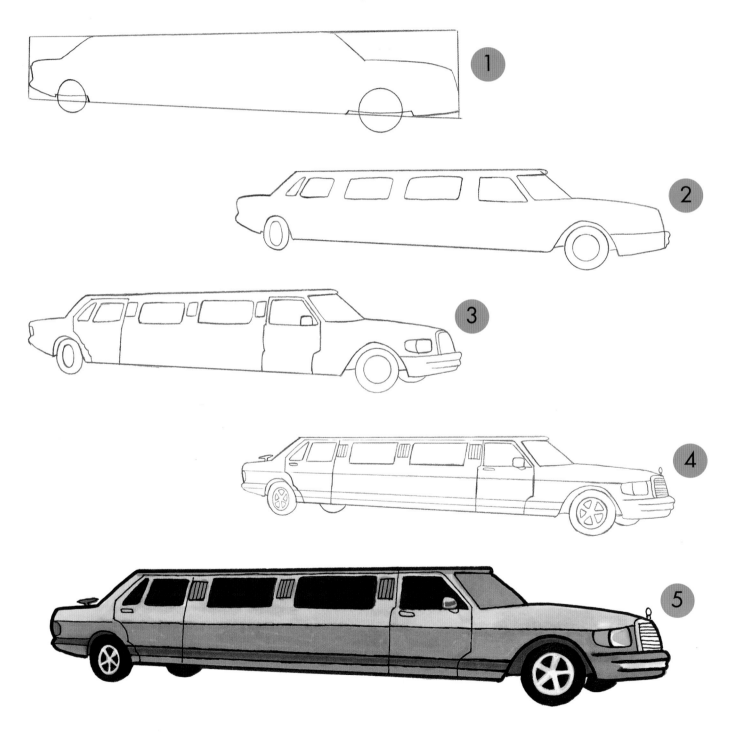

Ice Cream Truck

The **tall, boxy** shape of this truck shouts ice cream! Use super-bright colors, and draw your favorite frozen treats!

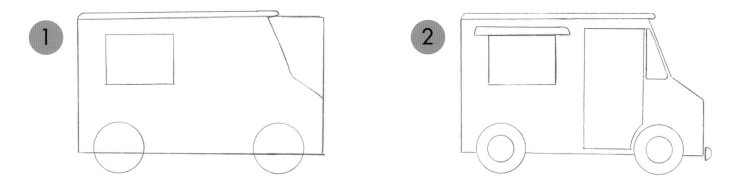

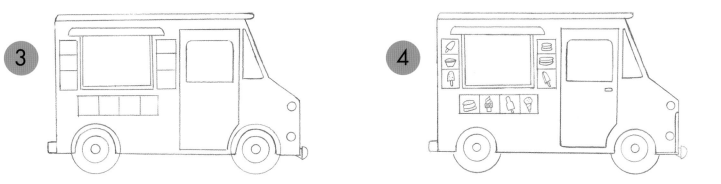

M1 Abrams Battle Tank

A 1,500-horsepower engine, three machine guns, and a 120 millimeter smoothbore cannon make this tank one tough trooper!

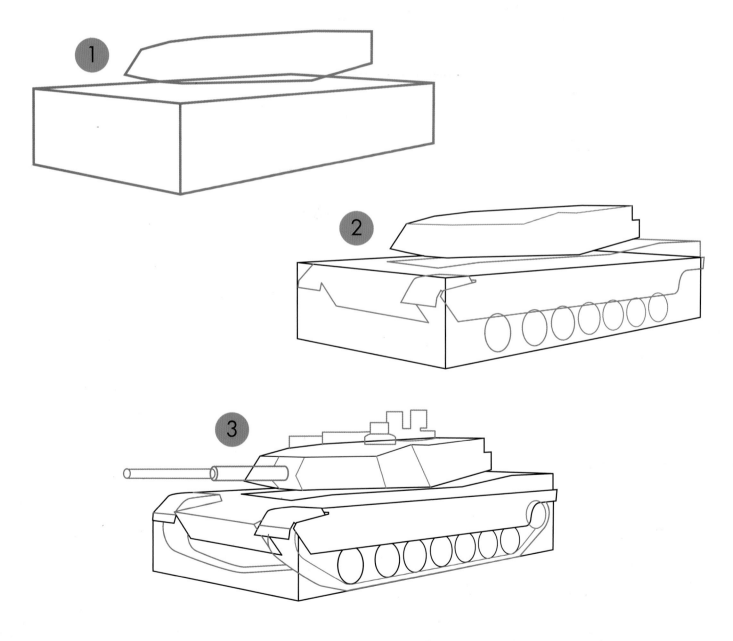

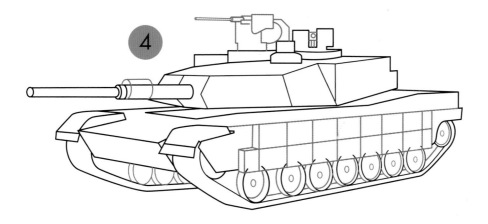

4

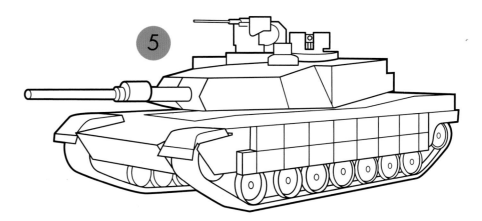

5

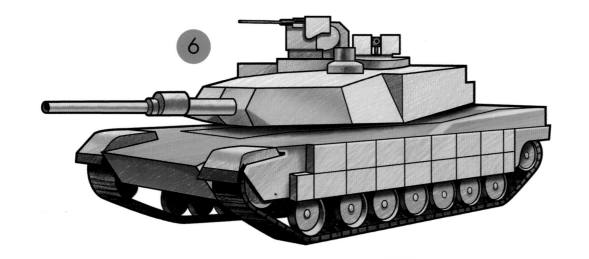

6

FUN FACT

The M1 is fitted with special ceramic and metal armor that protects it from anti-tank weapons. In fact, this battle tank is strong enough to survive a nuclear explosion!

Dump Truck

This **powerful** vehicle has a broad, **deep bed** that holds heavy loads, so the truck needs very large wheels and a solid frame.

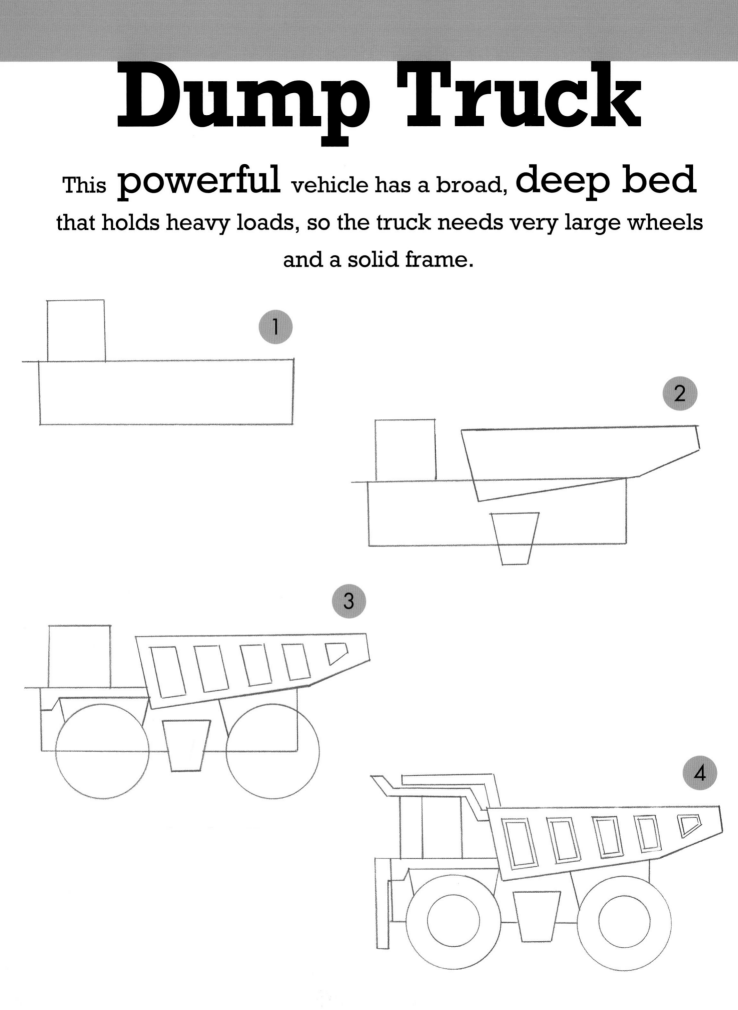

5

6

7

The first dump trucks appeared in the early 1900s; they were made to haul small loads that people alone couldn't move. Over time, dump trucks have become so large and powerful that they can easily carry loads as heavy as a large house!

Riverboat

This boat uses **steam** power and large **paddles** to operate. A flat bottom helps it steer in shallow water.

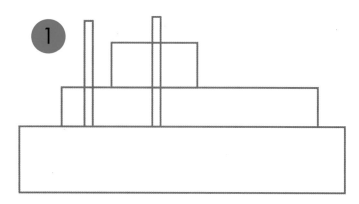

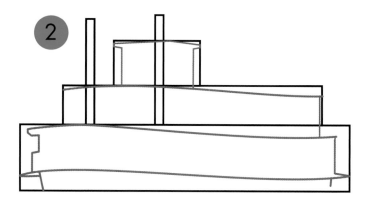

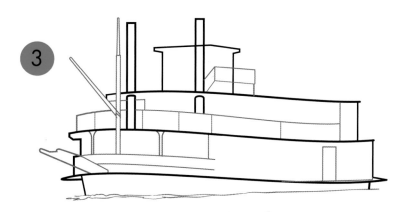

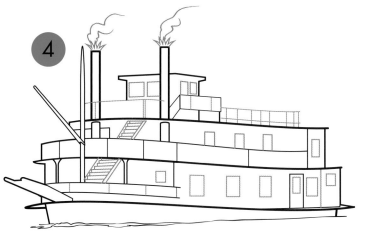

In the late 1800s, Mark Twain piloted a riverboat and wrote about his experiences in a book called *Life on the Mississippi.* There are few riverboats on the Mississippi River today; their engines often exploded, so most were destroyed.

Airborne Warning & Control System (AWACS)

An AWACS is a **radar dish** covered in a special damage-resistant case that attaches to the top of an aircraft.

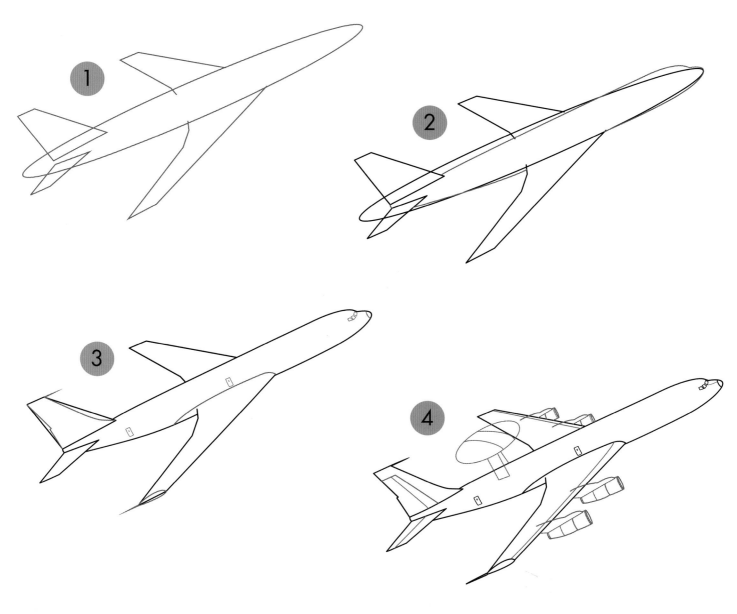

5

6

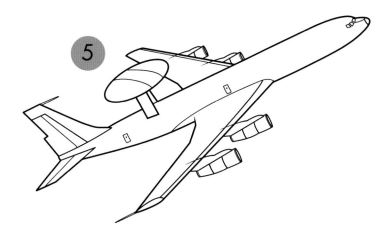

Airborne radars can detect enemy operations up to 250 miles away, as well as high up in the stratosphere. They can track airplanes, ships, and cruise missiles. They are used by many different countries and can also be attached to helicopters.

High Mobility Multipurpose Wheeled Vehicle (HUMVEE)

Before it became a consumer **sport-utility** vehicle, this diesel-fueled machine was used for military purposes.

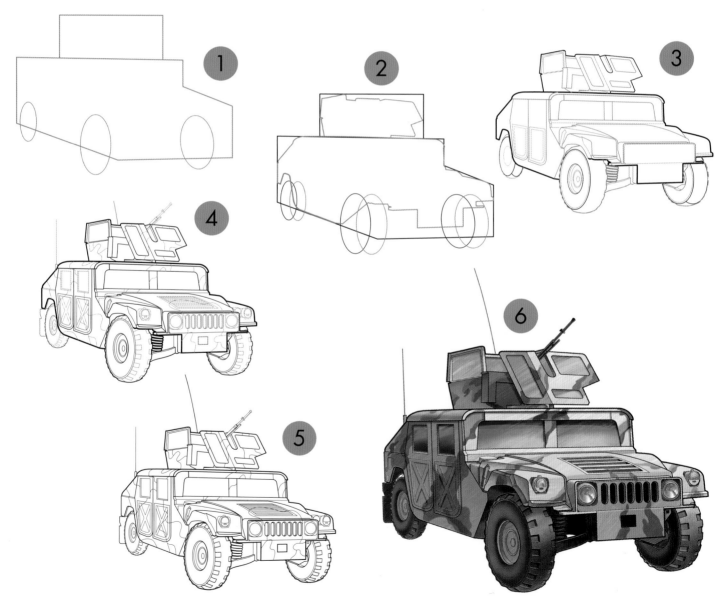

Heavy Expanded Mobility Tactical Truck (HEMTT)

Nicknamed the **"dragon wagon,"** this eight-wheel diesel truck can carry supplies, fuel tanks, and large artillery.

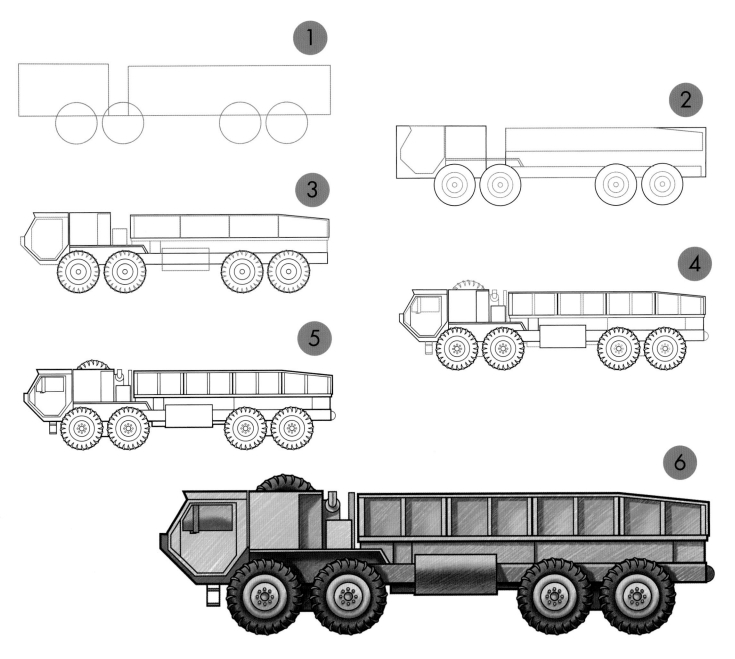

F-16

This single-engine, single-pilot **fighter jet** is small, light, quick, and it flies at supersonic, neck-breaking speeds!

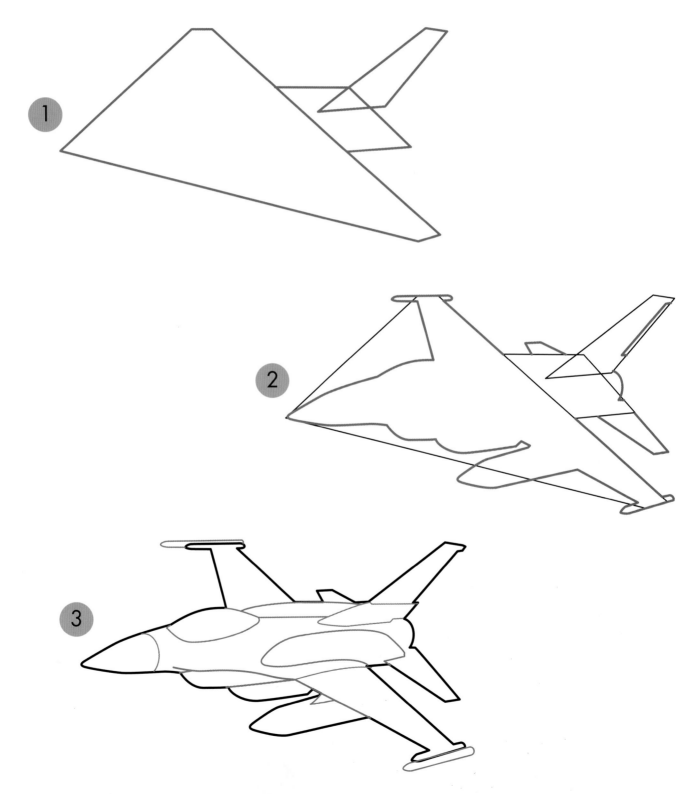

4

5

6

The F-16 comes fully loaded with an M61 Gatling-style gun. This piece of deadly artillery features a six-barrel 20 millimeter cannon that fires 6,000 rounds per minute. The gun rapidly spins in a circle, which allows it to fire continuously without reloading.

Cargo Ship

Powered by a **diesel** engine, this **massive** vessel transports cargo to shipping ports all over the world.

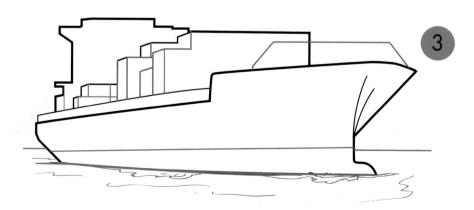

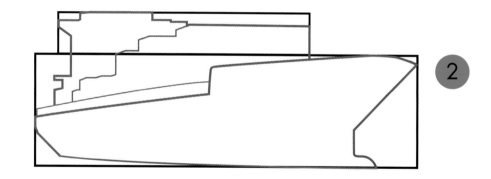

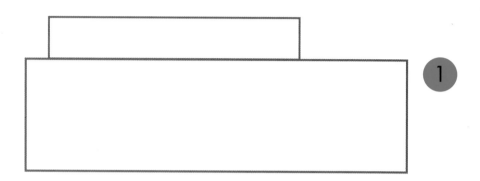

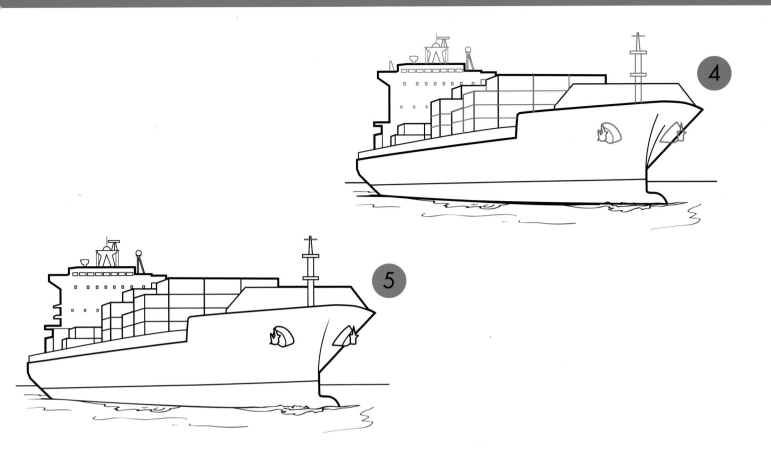

4

5

6

FUN FACT

Cargo ships carry goods in large steel containers stacked on top of each other—as many as 15,000 containers stacked 60 feet above deck! Giant cranes move the containers on and off the ships; then they place them onto trains and semi-trucks to travel to their land destinations.

Ambulance

When you color this **emergency vehicle**,
use bright colors so it really stands out when
it screams down the road.

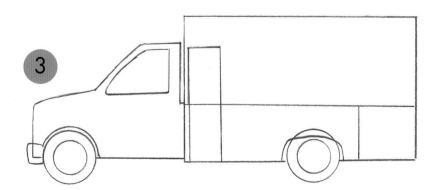

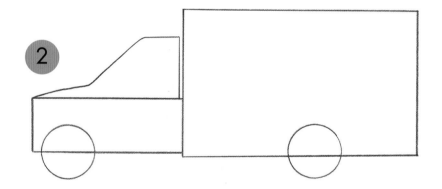

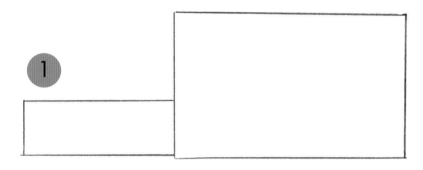

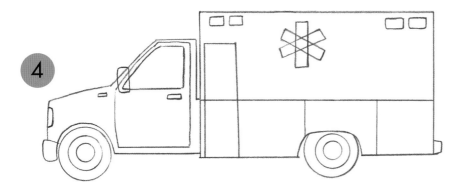

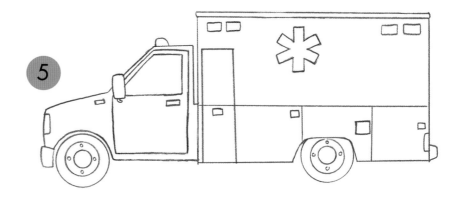

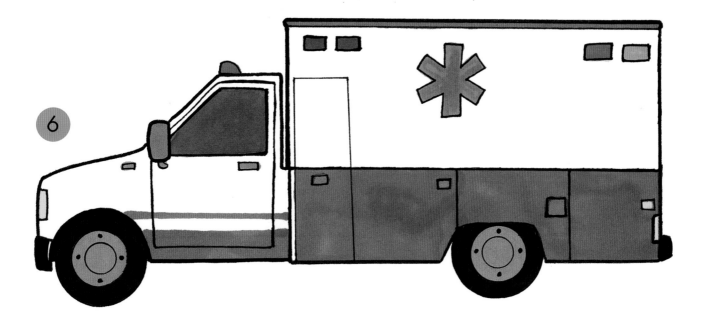

Tandem-Rotor Heavy-Lift Helicopter

This **combat** helicopter can **transport**

44 soldiers and travel more than 330 miles in a single trip.

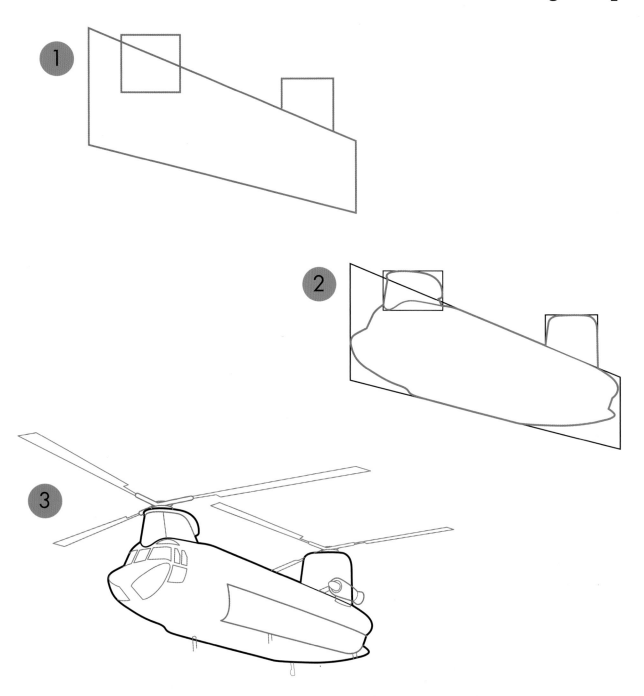

4

5

6

FUN FACT

This muscular helicopter is strong enough to carry two 5,000-pound HUMVEEs—the vehicles drive right onto the craft through its rear ramp. Three cargo hooks attached to its underside allow it to haul up to 26,000 pounds!

Glossary

Artillery: 1) Large firearms used in land warfare. 2) A branch of an army that uses artillery.

Armor: A shield or covering for the body that helps provide protection from bullets, projectiles, and shrapnel. 2) A protective layer or shield applied to the outer surface of a vehicle or machine.

Canal: A man-made water passage.

Cargo: The goods or merchandise transported by a ship, vehicle, or airplane.

Chauffeur: A person employed to transport passengers in an automobile.

Combat mission: A military operation in which the goal is to capture or defend people, objects, or territory.

Four-wheel drive: A transmission system that powers all four wheels of a vehicle.

Infantry: 1) Soldiers trained and equipped to engage in combat on foot. 2) A branch of an army made up of soldiers.

Twin-propeller plane: A plane with an engine that spins two propellers in opposite directions.

Missile: A weapon that is thrown or propelled at a target.

Night vision: In the military, refers to technology such as special goggles that enable its operator to see clearly in the dark or dim light.

Nuclear reactor: A device that initiates controlled nuclear chain reactions known as "fission," which in turn releases heat and creates energy.

Radar: A detection system composed of a transmitter and receiver that employs radio waves to locate ships, aircraft, and other objects.

Rotor: In an aircraft, a system of rotating airfoils that creates lift.

Stealth: Technology that makes it difficult to detect a moving vehicle's radar, sound, and heat emissions.